W9-AXY-777

FUNNY, FUNNIER AND FUNNIEST JOKE BOOK FOR KIDS...

and grownups who act like kids!

sf

SMITH FREEMAN Publishing

Funny, Funnier and Funniest Joke Book for Kids...

Cover design by Kim Russell | Wahoo Designs

ISBN 978-0-9986529-9-3

Table of Contents

Some Questions and Funny Answers About Animals

What kind of machine is best for lifting pigs?

A pork-lift.

What kind of vehicles do skunks drive?

Odor-cycles.

What do you give a pig with a rash?

Oinkment.

What kind of insect can you wear?

A yellow jacket.

What did the tired horse do at night?

It hit the hay.

What kind of cat should you never play games with?

A cheetah!

What did the judge say when the skunk walked into the courtroom?

Odor in the court!

Why did the policeman give the sheep a ticket?

He was a baaaaaaaaad driver.

What is more amazing than a talking dog?

A spelling bee.

Where do gorillas like to work out?

The jungle gym.

What do you call a lion at the South Pole?

Lost.

Why did the police arrest the snail?

Because he was found at the scene of the slime.

Which animal can't stop talking during class?

A yak.

How did the rancher count his cattle?

On a cow-culator.

What kind of medicine do ants take?

Ant-i-biotics.

How do you start a turtle race?

"Ready, set, slow!"

Where do squirrels store their food?

In the pan-tree.

Why didn't the skunk buy anything at the mall?

**He only had one cent
and it was bad.**

What happened to the frog's car?

It was toad.

How long was the hamster's workout?

Wheel-ie long.

Where do termites like to go on vacation?

Hollywood.

What does a gorilla wear when it cooks?

An ape-ron.

What animal can jump higher than a house?

All of them. Houses can't jump.

What do you call an easy-going rabbit?

Hoppy-go-lucky.

What do you call a snake who works for the government ?

A civil serpent.

What kind of school does a giraffe go to?

High school.

What's the scariest horse in the world?

A nightmare.

How do scientists freshen their breath?

With experi-mints.

Why was the young ant so confused?

Because all his uncles were ants.

What do you call a gorilla who plays golf?

Hairy Putter.

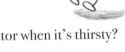

Where do funny frogs sit?

On silly pads.

What do you give an alligator when it's thirsty?

Gatorade.

What do you get when you cross a shellfish
and a rabbit?

The Oyster Bunny

What did the frog order for lunch?

French flies and a large croak.

Why couldn't the pony sing?

Because she was a little hoarse.

What does a goat eat for breakfast?

Goatmeal.

How do you stop a skunk from smelling?

You hold his nose.

What did the round bunny say to the square bunny?

"You're not from a round hare."

Why can you never trust the smartest animal in the world?

Because it's a cheetah.

Why do mother kangaroos hate rainy days?

Because their children have to play inside.

What do you call a very big ant?

A gi-ant.

What do you call a baby monkey?

A chimp off the old block.

Where do mice park their boats?

At the hickory dickory dock.

What do you call a rabbit that's really cool?

A hip hopper.

Why did the porcupine win every game?

He always had the most points.

What do you call a thieving alligator?

A crookodile.

What do you call a bear with no teeth?

A gummy bear.

About the Weather

What's the difference between weather and climate?

You can't weather a tree, but you can climate.

What do clouds wear when it's raining?

Thunderwear.

What do snowmen eat for breakfast?

Snowflakes.

How do hurricanes see?

With one eye.

Where do snowmen dance?

At the snowball.

What do clouds wear in their hair?

Rainbows.

What did the breeze say to the window screen?

"Just passing through."

What do you call a warm snowman?

Water.

Jokes and Riddles
About Ducks and Dinosaurs

What time did the duck wake up?

At the quack of dawn.

Why was the dinosaur afraid to go to the library?

Because his books were millions of years overdue.

What do you call a dinosaur that's about to about to tell a funny joke?

Pre-hysterical.

What do you get when dinosaurs crash their cars?

Tyrannosaurus wrecks.

What's the main difference between a duck and George Washington?

One has a bill on his face and the other has his face on a bill.

What did the dinosaur say after the car crash?

"I'm-so-saurus!"

What's a duck's favorite meal?

Soup and quackers.

Boy #1: "I wish I had enough money to buy a dinosaur."

Boy #2: "What would you do with a dinosaur?"

Boy #1: "Who wants a dinosaur? I just want the money!"

When is a duck not a duck?

When it's afloat.

How many dinosaurs can fit in an empty box?

One. After that, the box isn't empty anymore.

How can you tell if there's a dinosaur in the refrigerator?

The door won't close.

Why did the duck become a spy?

Because he was good at quacking codes.

What should you do if you find a dinosaur
in your bed?

Find somewhere else to sleep.

What do you call a T. rex wearing cowboy boots and
a 10-gallon hat?

Tyrannosaurus Tex.

How do you know if there's a dinosaur under
your bed?

Your nose keeps hitting the ceiling.

What do you get if you cross a pig with a dinosaur?

Jurassic Pork.

What do you call a crate filled with ducks?

A box of quackers.

Student #1 "What family does T. Rex belong to?"

Student #2: "I don't think any families in our
neighborhood have one."

Doctors and Dentists

Boy: "Doctor, doctor, my sister is invisible."

Doctor: "What sister?"

Patient: "Doctor, my Legos are broken. What do you recommend?"

Doctor: "Plastic surgery."

Patient: "Doctor, I have a weak back."

Doctor: "When did you first notice the problem?"

Patient: "Oh, about a week back."

What did the judge say to the dentist?

"Do you swear to pull the tooth, the whole tooth and nothing but the tooth?"

Doctor: "Why do you look so tired?"

Patient: "I knew I had a doctor's appointment, so I stayed up all night studying for my blood test."

Patient: "Doctor, I have a carrot growing out of my ear."

Doctor: "How could that have happened?"

Patient: "I don't know. I planted celery."

Patient: "Doctor, I think I broke my arm in two places."

Doctor: "Well, don't go back to those places."

Why did the pie crust go to the dentist?

It needed a filling.

Patient: "Doctor, last night I had a bad dream. I dreamed there was a door with a sign on it. I pushed and pushed, but the door wouldn't open."

Doctor: "That's interesting. What did the sign say?"

Patient: "Pull."

When does a doctor get mad?

When he runs out of patients!

A man went to the doctor and said, "I keep thinking I'm a church bell." The doctor said, "Take two aspirin, and if it doesn't work, give me a ring in the morning."

Patient: "Doctor, there must be something wrong with me. Sometimes, I think that I'm a dog."

Doctor: "Sit down on the couch and we'll talk about it."

Patient: "But I'm not allowed on the couch."

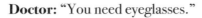

Doctor: "You need eyeglasses."

Patient: "How can you tell?"

Doctor: "Because you're talking to my skeleton model. I'm over here."

Doctor: "Nurse, did you take the patient's temperature?"

Nurse: "No. Is it missing?"

Patient #1: "I've been seeing spots all day."

Patient #2: "Did you see the eye doctor?"

Patient #1: "No, just spots."

What do dentists call their x-rays?

Toothpicks.

Patient: "Doctor, I think I'm shrinking."

Doctor: "Calm down. You'll just have to be a little patient."

Why did the king go to the dentist?

To get his teeth crowned!

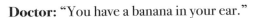

What time do you go to the dentist?

Tooth-hurty.

Doctor: "You have a banana in your ear."

Patient: "I can't hear you. I have a banana in my ear."

What did the dentist say to the computer?

"This won't hurt a byte."

What does a dentist do on a roller coaster?

He braces himself.

Patient: "Doctor, I have yellow teeth, what should I do?"

Dentist: "Wear a brown tie."

Mother: "Do you feel better now that you've gone to the dentist?"

Boy: "I sure do. He wasn't in."

What did the dentist say to the golfer?

"You have a hole in one."

What do you call a dentist in the army?

A drill sergeant.

About Dogs

What is the first thing a dog learns in school?

The arf-a-bet.

What did the spy name his dog?

Snoopy.

Boy #1: "My dog chases everybody on a bicycle. What should I do?"

Boy #2: "Take away his bicycle!"

What do you give a dog with a fever?

Mustard. It's the best thing for a hot dog.

What kind of dog is best with babies?

A baby setter.

Where do dogs refuse to shop?

At the flea market.

Where do dogs park their cars?

In a barking lot.

Why did the dog get kicked out of the choir?

It kept singing off key.

What happened when the dog ate the clock?

It got lots of ticks.

Boy: "A dog bit my leg this morning."

Nurse: "Did you put anything on it?"

Boy: "No, he liked it plain."

What did the dog say when he sat down on sandpaper?

"Ruff!"

What kind of dog always runs a fever?

A hot dog!

Why did the dog leap for joy?

Joy was his owner.

What time would it be if you saw 10 dogs chasing a cat up a tree?

Ten after one.

What goes tick-tock, bow-wow, tick-tock, bow-wow?

A watch dog.

Boy #1: "Did you like the story about the dog that ran three miles just to pick up a stick?"

Boy #2: "No, I thought it was a little far-fetched."

Fun with Fish!

Boy #1: "Did you give your goldfish water today?"

Boy #2: "No. They didn't finish the water I gave them yesterday."

What do jellyfish eat for breakfast?

Floatmeal.

Why are some fish at the bottom of the ocean?

Because they dropped out of school.

What happened when the shark became famous?

He turned into a starfish.

Where do fish keep their money?

In a river bank!

What fish only swims at night?

A starfish.

Which book is every fish's favorite?

Huckleberry Fin.

How do you communicate with a fish?

You drop it a line.

Why don't fish use computers?

They're afraid of getting snagged online or getting caught up in the Net.

Why did the young fish stay home from school?

He was feeling a little under the water.

Are shellfish warm?

No, they're clammy.

Where do the fish like to go on vacation?

Finland

Why are fish bad at basketball?

They're afraid of the nets.

Which whale is the saddest?

The blue whale.

Which fish is the funniest?

The cartoon-a.

What do you call a whale that can't keep a secret?

A blubber-mouth.

Why did the dolphin cross the bay?

To get to the other tide!

Why do fish in the ocean stay so healthy?

Because they always get plenty of "Vitamin Sea."

How do you make a goldfish old?

Take away the g!

Where does the army keep its fish?

In a tank.

What do fish use to calm their babies?

A bassifier.

What do you say to a blue whale?

"Cheer up."

35

Does a dolphin ever do something by accident?

No, it does everything on porpoise.

What kind of gum do whales chew?

Blubber gum.

What club do young whales like to join?

The Boy Spouts

What are the easiest animals to weigh?

Fish, because they have scales.

Why should you never tell a joke while ice fishing?

Because the ice might crack up.